This book belongs to

Jessica Bartlett

I'm VERY special
to God!

When MARY Was Little

Written by Sally Wilkins

Illustrated by
Mary Joseph Peterson, FSP

Pauline
BOOKS & MEDIA
BOSTON

Library of Congress Cataloging-in-Publication Data

Wilkins, Sally.
    When Mary was little / written by Sally Wilkins ; illustrated by Mary
Joseph Peterson.
        p. cm.
    Summary: Simple text imagines the experiences and actions of
Mary, the mother of Jesus, as a child, including helping her parents,
praying, and playing with friends, and relates them to those of a
modern child.
    ISBN 0-8198-8294-1
    1. Mary, Blessed Virgin, Saint—Childhood and youth—Juvenile
literature. [1. Mary, Blessed Virgin, Saint—Childhood and
youth. 2. Saints.] I. Peterson, Mary Joseph, ill.   II. Title.
BT607.W55   1999
232.91—dc21   99–17350
                                                                   CIP

By the same author:
When Jesus Was Little

Printed and published in the U.S.A. by Pauline Books & Media,
50 Saint Pauls Avenue, Boston MA 02130-3491.

www.pauline.org

Pauline Books & Media is the publishing house of the Daughters of
St. Paul, an international congregation of women religious serving
the Church with the communications media.

2 3 4 5 6 7 8   05 04 03 02 01 00

Word List
(thirty-nine words)

and	I	sew
clothes	just	shared
combed		she
	learned	shopping
do	like	
	little	things
family	lived	to
father	loved	too
friends		toys
	Mary	
God	mother	was
God's		wash
	other	went
hair		when
helped	people	with
her	played	
house	pray	

For Parent/Child Sharing

This book is about Mary, the mother of Jesus. Jesus is God. And so Mary is God's mother.

Out of all the women in the world, God chose Mary to be the mother of his son. Mary had to be very, very good. God never let Mary be without his friendship. In God's special plan, Mary was born without original sin. This was something wonderful!

Mary had to grow up just like you. Mary grew up in a family. Mary and her family were Jewish. They loved, honored and obeyed God as the Jewish religion teaches.

When Mary was little, she did many of the same things that you do. Can you guess what they are? This book will tell you about some.

Mary is our Blessed Mother. She takes care of us now from heaven. Mary loves you! Mary will help you love her son Jesus more and more!

When Mary was little
she lived with her family.

Just like I do.

When Mary was little she loved and helped her mother and father.

Just like I do.

When Mary was little
she combed her hair.

Just like I do.

When Mary was little
she learned to pray.

Just like I do.

When Mary was little
she helped wash clothes.

Just like I do.

When Mary was little
she loved other
people.

Just like I do.

When Mary was little
she learned to sew.

Just like I do.

21

When Mary was little
she played with toys.

Just like I do.

When Mary was little
she shared her things.

Just like I do.

When Mary was little
she went shopping.

Just like I do.

When Mary was little
she played with her friends.

Just like I do.

When Mary was little she loved God and went to God's house.

I do, too!

BOOKS & MEDIA

The Daughters of St. Paul operate book and media centers at the following addresses. Visit, call or write the one nearest you today, or find us on the World Wide Web, www.pauline.org

California
3908 Sepulveda Blvd., Culver City, CA 90230; 310-397-8676
5945 Balboa Ave., San Diego, CA 92111; 858-565-9181
46 Geary Street, San Francisco, CA 94108; 415-781-5180

Florida
145 S.W. 107th Ave., Miami, FL 33174; 305-559-6715

Hawaii
1143 Bishop Street, Honolulu, HI 96813; 808-521-2731
Neighbor Islands call: 800-259-8463

Illinois
172 North Michigan Ave., Chicago, IL 60601; 312-346-4228

Louisiana
4403 Veterans Memorial Blvd., Metairie, LA 70006; 504-887-7631

Massachusetts
Rte. 1, 885 Providence Hwy., Dedham, MA 02026; 781-326-5385

Missouri
9804 Watson Rd., St. Louis, MO 63126; 314-965-3512

New Jersey
561 U.S. Route 1, Wick Plaza, Edison, NJ 08817; 732-572-1200

New York
150 East 52nd Street, New York, NY 10022; 212-754-1110
78 Fort Place, Staten Island, NY 10301; 718-447-5071

Ohio
2105 Ontario Street, Cleveland, OH 44115; 216-621-9427

Pennsylvania
9171-A Roosevelt Blvd., Philadelphia, PA 19114; 215-676-9494

South Carolina
243 King Street, Charleston, SC 29401; 843-577-0175

Tennessee
4811 Poplar Ave., Memphis, TN 38117; 901-761-2987

Texas
114 Main Plaza, San Antonio, TX 78205; 210-224-8101

Virginia
1025 King Street, Alexandria, VA 22314; 703-549-3806

Canada
3022 Dufferin Street, Toronto, Ontario, Canada M6B 3T5; 416-781-9131
1155 Yonge Street, Toronto, Ontario, Canada M4T 1W2; 416-934-3440

¡También somos su fuente para libros, videos y música en español!